Monographic Journals of the Near East *Afroasiatic Linguistics* 2/7 (June 1975)

*This paper is part of the
Proceedings
of the
First North-American Conference on Semitic Linguistic
Santa Barbara, California
March 24-25, 1973*

SYSTEMATIC VS. AUTONOMOUS PHONEMICS AND THE HEBREW GRAPHEME dagesh

Joseph L. Malone

Barnard College and Columbia University

An early established tenet of generative phonologists was that the SYSTEMATIC PHONEME should replace the neo-Bloomfieldian AUTONOMOUS PHONEME in phonological theory, this being a gratuitous hypostatization frequently making it impossible to state phonological patterning in fully general form. This was early demonstrated by Robert Lees and Morris Halle in the now classical cases of Turkish and Russian devoicing. The present paper argues that for Tiberian Hebrew, ALTHOUGH autonomous phonemic analysis (§2) and systematic phonemic analysis (§3) clash in a considerably more radical way than do the above cases (§4), NEVERTHELESS the distribution of the grapheme *dagesh* is interpretable only pursuant to the autonomous phonemic analysis (§5). A solution is suggested to this apparent paradox (§6).

TABLE OF CONTENTS

1. INTRODUCTION

An early established and long maintained tenet of generative phonologists was that the SYSTEMATIC PHONEME (hereinafter S-PHONEME) should replace the neo-Bloomfieldian AUTONOMOUS PHONEME (hereinafter A-PHONEME) in phonological theory, the A-phoneme being not only a gratuitous hypostatization but indeed one frequently making it difficult or impossible to state phonological patterning in fully general form. The cogency of this view was early demonstrated by Lees (1957:389f) and Halle (1959 [reprinted as 1971]:22f) in the now-classic cases of Turkish and Russian devoicing. However the generativists never succeeded in converting all phonologists of all stripes to condemnation of the A-phoneme, and not only has a respectable body of eristic literature accumulated on the topic (notable the Chomsky-Halle-Householder series in the inaugural issues of the *Journal of Linguistics*, now reprinted in Makkai 1972:442-90; cf. also §4.2 below), but recently some generative phonologists themselves have proposed that a unit akin if not identical to the A-phoneme be repatriated to phonological theory (in addition to those cited in §6.1, at least also Wang 1968:707 note 19).

This paper argues that in the case of Tiberian Hebrew ALTHOUGH A-phonemic analysis (§2) and S-phonemic analysis (§3) clash in a considerably more radical way than do the classic cases of Turkish and Russian cited above (§4), NEVERTHELESS the orthographic distribution of the grapheme *dagesh* is interpretable only pursuant to the A-phonemic analysis (§5). The paper ends with discussion and suggested resolution of this apparent paradox (§6).[1]

2. THE AUTONOMOUS PHONEMIC ANALYSIS

If the forms of (1) and (2)[2] are taken as representative of the phonetic distribution of Tiberian Hebrew consonants exclusive of what are traditionally called the *begedkefet* consonants, i.e. the non-pharyngealized non-rilled obstruents [p,t,k,b,d,g,f,θ,x,v,ð,γ], and exclusive of the low glides [ʔ,h,ʕ,ḥ] and low liquid [r], then the following conclusion must be reached concerning the A-phonemic status of gemination of the pharyngealized stops [ṭ,q], the rilled spirants [s,ṣ,z,š,ś], the nasals [m,n], the non-low glides [y,w], and the non-low liquid [l]: although gemination is restricted to intervocalic position, it is in that position contrastive with simple consonantism (see (1e) and (2e)) and thus for any non-*begedkefet* non-low C, [C] is A-phonemically distince from [CC], ergo the opposition /C/ ≠ /CC/.[3]

---

[1]The object language, Tiberian Hebrew, is that form of Hebrew canonicized, for reading and cantillation of the Bible, by the Masoretes (rabbinical scribe-philologists) centered in Tiberias (on the Sea of Galilee) in the latter part of the first millenium CE (= AD); see the references in notes 17 and 18.

[2]Entries of (1-5) are organized as follows from left to right. [ ] = a BROAD-PHONETIC INTERPRETATION (largely following Bauer & Leander 1962, but with segment-symbols more conventional to American linguistics; see also note 15), with the segment in focus underscored, of the next-following TRANSLITERATION, in < >, of the BIBLICAL ORTHOGRAPHIC FORM, following Kittel et al. (1971), which in all but three cases (see next sentence) is stripped only of its accentual graphemes where <:> = the grapheme (≠ phone(me)!) *schwa*, <°> = *dagesh*, <ˌ> *metheg*, < ̣ ˌ ̀ > = the accentual graphemes *munaḥ*, *silluq*, and *azla* resp. A gloss. The Biblical source (G = Genesis, D = Deuteronomy, S = Samuel, K = Kings, E = Ezekiel).

[3]Passim below, use of the term "gemination" or the representation CC should be understood in accordance with notes 15 and 16a. Throughout the body of the paper two A-phonemic grades of vowel quantity will be assumed, NORMAL GRADE /V/ (occasionally symbolized by V̆ to forfend

(1) Simple non-*begedkefet* non-low consonants.

(a)#___V. [nɔ̄hɔ̄r] < nɔhɔr > 'river' (Numbers 24:6).
[rɔ̄xāv] < rɔkab > 'he rode' (Esther 6:8).

(b)#___C.[4] [ṣ̌tāyim] < š:t̊ayim > 'two(fe.)' (G 5:18).

(c)V___#. [zɔ̄mām] < zɔmam > 'he plotted (mischief)' (D 19:19).
[nɔ̄fāl] < nɔpal > 'he fell' (Judges 5:27).
[qɛ́rɛn] < qɛ̧rɛn > (*munaḥ*) 'horn' (I S 16:13).

---

confusion with the generic use of *V* for "any vowel") and LONG GRADE /V̄/, the question of a possible REDUCED GRADE /V̆/ being left moot. The assumption of an A-phonemic normal ≠ long opposition is by no means uncontroversial, however, and it is likely enough that prosodic change had effaced this distinction on the A-phonemic level sometime before the Tiberian stage (cf. Malone 1972: note 2 and references), in which case the phonetic interpretations of vowel quantity in (1-2) and passim would have to be adjusted. This eventuality would not only be *un*damaging to the arguments of this section, but in fact would simplify their statement. However on the positive assumption of a /V/ ≠ /V̄/ opposition, care must be taken to demonstrate the A-phonemic independence from this of the hypothesized /C/ ≠ /CC/ (simplex ≠ geminate) opposition since the latter is predictable, either in terms of the former or otherwise, IN ALL ENVIRONMENTS EXCEPT IMMEDIATELY FOLLOWING A STRESSED VOWEL. Thus the intervocalic oppositional triplet [tirʔɛ̄́nɔ̄], [wattɛ́mɛr], and [wə̆naᶜăśɛ̄́nnɔ̄] adduced in (1e) and (2e) was specifically selected for its relative cogency, in which vein the following points should be considered. (i) Whereas TONIC LENGTHENING affects both verbal and nominal words (the latter including object-suffixed verbs as a special case, the likely crucial reason being given by Kuryłowicz 1959:125-7 relevant to which the hypothesis of Brame 1971:567f seems promising) in the sentence-intonationally most prominent positions traditionally called PAUSE normally signaled by the accentual graphemes *silluq* and *athnaḥ*, and (ii) whereas tonic lengthening affects no word in intonationally least prominent PROCLITIC position signaled by the grapheme *maqqef*, yet (iii) in intonational positions of intermediate prominence tonic lengthening is common only in nominal, not in verbal words. (iv) In particular, in positions of second-lowest prominence, orthographically signaled by CONJUNCTIVE ACCENTS, verbs never evidence tonic lengthening (the few apparent cases being probably spurious; Bergsträsser 1962:I160). (v) Hence conjunctive-accented verbs like (1e) < watɛ̊̀mɛr > (with the accent *azla* ̀) are to be interpreted as [wattɛ́mɛr] rather than §[wattɛ̄́mɛr] (§ marks synchronic non-existence or non-attestation, * being reserved for reconstructions) because tonic lengthening is excluded and (vi) because forms like this patently derive historically from antecedents with short tonic vowel **wattámr*, and moreover (vii) in consideration of evidence from the nominal system that an actual tonic-lengthened reflex of **wattámr* should appear as §[wattɔ̄́mɛr]. (Cf. pausal < qɔ̧rɛn >, with *athnaḥ*, ̂ , [qɔ̄́rɛn] 'horn' in I Chronicles 25:5 vs. conjunctive < qɛ̧rɛn >, with *munaḥ* ̧ , [qɛ́rɛn] in (1c) above. Admittedly the force of (vii) *per se* is tempered by the possibility of occasional pausal nominals like < wɔmɛ̧lɛk: > 'and (the) king' in I K 21:10 which some [e.g. Bauer & Leander 1962:185] interpret as tonic-lengthened [mɛ̄́lɛx]). (viii) While it is not clear whether pausal < w:naᶜăśɛ̧̊nɔh > (2e), with *silluq*, should be interpreted as [wə̆naᶜăśɛ̄́nnɔ̄] or [wə̆naᶜăśɛ́nnɔ̄], since immediately following gemination frequently counteracts tonic lengthening, yet in either event pausal < t̊ir:ʔɛ̧ynɔh > (1e) is surely [tirʔɛ̄́nɔ̄] even independently of (i) above, since this [ɛ̄] < **ay*, and monophthongized diphthongs are always long in Hebrew regardless of intonational position. (ix) Ergo [wattɛ́mɛr] vs. [wə̆naᶜăśɛ̄́nnɔ̄] (or [wə̆naᶜăśɛ́nnɔ̄]) vs. [tirʔɛ̄́nɔ̄] demonstrate the independence of /C/ ≠ /CC/ from immediately preceding /V̄/ ≠ /V/.

[4] Filled only by [š-] of [št-] in feminine forms of the cardinal numeral 'two'. But not all accept this phonetic interpretation of < š:t- >.

(d)C___#. [qōšṯ][5] < qoš:ṭ: > 'truth' (Proverbs 22:21).

(e)V___V. [tirʔē̱nō̱] < tir:ʔęynoh > (*silluq*) 'they(fe.) shall see' (Isaiah 17:7).

[wattē̱mɛr] < watẽmɛr > (*azla*) 'and she has changed' (E 5:6).

(f)V___C. [ʔɛnhō̱γə̆xō] < ʔɛn:hǫg:kɔ > 'I would lead thee' (Song of Songs 8:2).

(g)C___V. [bə̆qarnō̱w] < b̊:qar:nɔyw > 'by his horns' (G 22:13).

(2) Geminate non-*begedkefet* non-low consonants.

Only (e)V___V. [tiqqóm] < tiq̊om > 'thou shalt avenge' (Leviticus 19:18).

[wə̆naᶜăsē̱nnō̱] (or [wə̆naᶜăsē̱nnō̱] (*silluq*)

< w:naᶜăsęn̊oh > 'we may do it' (D 30:13).

[hannōhō̱r] < han̊ɔhɔr > 'the river' (G 2:13).

[zimmō̱] < zim̊ɔh > 'mischief' (Psalms 26:10).

To what degree can this opposition be extended to the remaining Tiberian consonants? In the cases *per se* of low [ʔ,h,ᶜ,ḥ,r] and *begedkefet* spirant [f,θ,x,v,ð,γ] the question cannot be posed, since these sounds do not occur geminated.[6] As for the *begedfeket* stops, though [p,t,k,b,d,g] occur as both simplices (3) and geminates (4), unlike the case of (1-2) there is not contrast but COMPLEMENTARY DISTRIBUTION in the crucial environment: the simplices never occur intervocalically (3e) while the geminates always do (4e).

(3) Simple *begedkefet* stops.

(a)#___V. [dō̱vō̱r] < d̊ɔbɔr > 'word' (G 44:18).

(b)#___C. - - -

(c)V___#. [yīḥad] < yiḥad̊: > 'let it rejoice' (Job 3:6).

(d)C___#. [nērd][5] < ner:d̊: > 'nard' (Song of Songs 4:14).

(e)V___V. - - -

(f)V___C. - - -

(g)C___V. [lə̆rixbō̱] < l:rik:b̊ɔh > 'for riding' (E 27:20).

[happirdō̱] < hap̊ir:d̊ɔh > 'the she-mule' (I K 1:33)

---

[5]Some interpret as paragogic [qōšṭə̆], [nērdə̆], and so for all presumed -CC forms; cf. Bergsträsser (1962:I 137).

[6]The assumption that *begedkefet* spirants never occur geminated depends on NOT interpreting forms like <rib:bowt > 'myriads' (D 33:17) as [rivvōθ], but rather as [rivə̆vōθ] or the like (following Kautzsch 1910:71; cf. also David K. Ḳimḥi's opinion, Chomsky 1952:21). In fact, I now suspect that [rivvōθ] is correct, but proceed in this paper on the contrary assumption because (i) defense of this controversial (in post-Masoretic times! See the reference to Ben Asher in Chomsky 1952:20) assumption would require detailed extraneous digression, and (ii) the admissibility of such clusters would not materially affect the arguments of this paper in any event. See also note 10.

(4) Geminate *begedkefet* stops.

Only (e)V___V. [yip̲p̲ṓl] < yip̊ol > 'it falls' (II S 17:12).
[had̲d̲ɔ̄vɔ̄́r] < had̊ɔbɔr > 'the word' (G 37:11).
[mid̲d̲ɔ̄́] < mid̊ɔh > 'measure' (Exodus 26:2).

Moreover the simplices manifest clear and systematic PHONETIC SIMILARITY pair-wise with their corresponding geminates; and though this relation is no less clearly and sytematically borne by the simplices to their corresponding spirants in (5), yet it will be seen that this phonetic similarity is disentitled by contrast in environments (c) and (g).

(5) Simple *begedkefet* spirants.

(a)#___V. - - -[7]
(b)#___C. - - -
(c)V___#. [happrɛ́ð̲] < hap̊ɛrɛd > 'the mule' (II S 18:9).
[yā́ḥað̲] < yaḥad > 'together' (Job 10:8).
(d)C___#. - - -
(e)V___V. [mɔ̄ð̲ā́ð] < mɔdad > 'he measured' (E 40:20).
[pə̆rɔ̄ð̲ī́m] < p̊:rɔdiym > 'mules' (II K 5:17).
[wɔ̄f̲ɛ́rɛð] < wɔpɛrɛd > 'and mules(s)' (I K 18:5).
(f)V___C. [mēḥɛð̲rṓ] < mẹḥɛd:row > 'from his chamber' (Joel 2:16).
(g)C___V. [pirð̲ēhɛ̄́m] < pir:deyhɛm > 'their mules' (Ezra 2:66).

(6) Geminate *begedkefet* spirants do not occur (but see note 6).

Hence A-phonemically the simple and geminate *begedfeket* stops may be paired off as co-allophones, gemination being predictable intervocalically, as in (7e-h). But an analogous solution is impossible in other consonants: by absolute non-occurrence in the case of the *begedkefet* spirants (7j) and the low consonants, and by contrast in the case of the remaining consonants (7a-d). Distributional skewages not solved by the analysis are left to phonotactic statement; e.g. (7j) (as well as (3b), (5d), etc.).

(7) The A-phonemic analysis in summary[8] (P,F,M stand respectively for any *begedkefet* stop, *begedkefet* spirant, any other C):

[7]Actually, the spirants in question do occur under most conditions in the subenvironment V#___V where the syntactic bond between the two words is relatively close (orthographically signaled by a conjunctive accent or *maqqef*); cf. Bergsträsser 1962:I §18. For simplicity's sake such cases are not considered in this paper, but their inclusion would not materially affect any aspect of the discussion.

[8]This analysis largely converges with that of Schramm (1964:see esp. 57), while that of Harris (1941; for an earlier stage of Hebrew but also valid for Tiberian in relevant respects) posits an independent lengthening phoneme /·/ and so views [MM] and [PP] as /M·/ and /P·/, the complementary distribution [PP] ~ [P] being apparently regarded as a structural coincidence. The analyses of Cantineau (1950) and Morag (1962) cannot usefully be brought into comparison, given both explicit differences in phonetic interpretation and implicit differences in phonemic theory.

(a) /M/ → [M] /everywhere. E.g. (1a) [n̲ɔ̄hɔ̄́r] ← /n̲ɔ̄hɔ̄́r/.

(b) /MM/ → [MM] /everywhere. E.g. (2e) [hann̲ɔ̄hɔ̄́r] ← /hann̲ɔ̄hɔ̄́r/.

(c) [tiqqóm] ← /tiqqóm/

(d) [zimmɔ̄́] ← /zimmɔ̄́/.

(e) /P/ → [PP] /V__V. E.g. (4e) [hadd̲ɔ̄vɔ̄́r] ← /had̲ɔ̄vɔ̄́r/.

(f) [yippól] ← /yipól/.

(g) [middɔ̄́] ← /midɔ̄́/.

(h) /P/ → [P] /elsewhere. E.g. (3a) [d̲əvɔ̄́r] ← /d̲əvɔ̄́r/.

(i) /F/ → [F] /elsewhere. E.g. (5g) [pirə̄ðēhḗm] ← /pirə̄ðēhḗm/.

(j) §/FF/, hence also §[FF], is phonotactically restricted (but see note 6).

3. THE SYSTEMATIC PHONEMIC ANALYSIS

3.1. Overview

It will be noted that the A-phonemic analysis of (7) functionally groups the *begedkefet* simple spirants ([F]) over against the corresponding stops irrespective of gemination ([P] ~ [PP]). But the closest analogous functional grouping dictated by an S-phonemic analysis must set the *begedkefet* geminate stops ([PP]) over against the corresponding simplices irrespective of spirantialization ([P] ~ [F]). Some of the relevant points will now be considered.

3.2. [P] ∿ [F]: Simple Stops Alternating with Simple Spirants

Tiberian morphophonology is pervaded with clear cases of postvocalic [F] alternating with [P] in other positions; e.g. from the inflectional and derivational paradigm of the noun stem glossing 'mule', note the postvocalic [ð] in (5c) [happḗrɛð] and (5e) [pə̆rɔ̄ðī́m] in alternation with the postconsonantal [d] in (3g) [happirdɔ̄́]. The alternational manifestation of the non-existence of §[FF] (A-phonemically noted as a phonotactic restriction in (7j)) may be seen in the invariance of [PP]: e.g. [pp] in (3g) [happirdɔ̄́] despite its postvocalic position; compare the expected appearance of the corresponding simplex spirant [f] postvocalically in (5e) [wɔ̄fḗrɛð] alternating with its simplex stop counterpart [p] initially (hence non-postvocalically) in (5e) [pə̆rɔ̄ðī́m].

The most straightforward way to capture these regularities S-phonemically is by (i) abrogating the phonetic distinction [P] ≠ [F] at the systematic phonemic level in favor of |P|, and (ii) formulating a phonological rule of SPIRANTALIZATION to the effect that:

(8) A non-pharyngealized simplex obstruent is rendered continuant (spirantalized) in postvocalic position.

But what of seeming exceptions to this rule like (3c) [yīḥad̲] on the one hand and (5g) [pirə̄ðēhḗm] on the other? As regards the former, suffice it here to say that the ilk of [yīḥad̲] is EXTREMELY RESTRICTED in Tiberian, and that whatever their eventual disposition the generality of (8) will remain intact.[9] As regards the latter, though the ilk of [pirə̄ðēhḗm] is EXTREMELY WIDESPREAD, such forms are only apparent exceptions to (8). On the contrary, it turns out that the [F] of such forms is indeed the product of (8), but

[9] For reasons not to be spelled out here, the solution I proposed for [yīḥad] in Malone (1969: 539(ii)) has grown highly suspicious, though the explanation proposed there for the other relevant forms (pp. 536-47) still holds whether one opts for my "A-rule" (p. 546) or the more orthodox generative-phonological rule (IIIa') (p. 542).

that the environmental vowel has been lost by the subsequent action of a rule of REDUCTION, itself of pervasive scope quite independently of the question of Spirantalization, to the effect that:

(9) A normal-grade open-syllabic vowel in any pretonic position is syncopated immediately following *V̌C*, and elsewhere weakened to ə̆.[10] Reduction is right-to-left[10a] iterative, i.e. in case there are two or more reduction-susceptible vowels, they are reduced seriatim in an order directly proportional to their relative proximity to the stress, the continued reducibility of each vowel being subject to cancelation by syllable-closure induced by prior Reduction in the adjacent syllable.

Thus in the case of [pirðēhḗm] we have:[11]

(10) (...)	|paradēhḗm|
(by 8)	para<u>ð</u>ēhḗm
(by 9)	parðēhḗm
(---)	[pirðēhḗm]

But granting the independence of Spirantalization and Reduction, is there any synchronic evidence INDEPENDENT OF SPIRANTALIZATION for the underlying presence of the vowel crucial to this rule in cases like [pirðēhḗm]? That is, might we not be engaging in fallacious inference from the particular (= the great number of clear cases of postvocalic Spirantalization, e.g. (5c,e)) to the universal (∴ *all* cases of Spirantalization must be postvocalic, hence [pirðēhḗm] must derive from an antecedent containing *Vd*)? In fact there is abundant alternational evidence, independent of Spirantalization and quite varied in character, for the synchronic existence of such vowels. In the specific case of [pirðēhḗm], the pertinent vowel is manifested phonetically as [ɔ̄] in the homoparadigmatic form (5e) [pə̆rɔ̄ðī́m] where it is preserved from Reduction by the prior action of PRETONIC LENGTHENING, itself an independently motivated rule of pervasive application:

(11) A normal-grade open-syllabic vowel immediately pretonic to a full-stressed syllable may be lengthened. This lengthening is nearly categorical in the case of *â*, and probably the norm for other values of *V*.

Thus in the case of [pə̆rɔ̄ðī́m] we have:

---

[10]However, if in the case of forms like < rib:bowt > the interpretation [rivə̆vōθ] is correct, then Reduction effects weakening to ə̆ rather than full syncope immediately following a *V̂C* whose C would by syncope form a cluster with an immediately following identical C. If on the other hand [rivvōθ] is correct, Reduction as stated in the text needs no adjustment.

[10a]That is, its movement is *regressive*. Thanks to Robert Hetzron for bringing to my attention this area of possible confusion to Semitists accustomed to the right-to-left direction of West Semitic writing.

[11]This and subsequent S-phonemic derivations are abbreviated and distorted for simplicity's and economy's sake: | | is not the actual systematic phonemic representation (which in the case of (10)--omitting diacritics, boundaries, brackets, etc.--should look something like |paradayhimma|) but rather a form already processed by as many rules as are neither dependent upon nor fed by the rules explicitly listed (8 and 9 in the case of 10). The class (possibly null) of such omitted rules is represented by (...) on the first line, while (---) on the last line similarly represents rules fed by one or more of the rules explicitly listed. For most of these omitted rules, cf. Malone (1972:§1.1 with references in note 2).

(12) (...) |paradī́m|
(8) paraðī́m
(11) parāðī́m
(9) pə̆rāðī́m
(---) [pə̆rɔ̄ðī́m]

A comparison of (10) and (12) reveals that the allo-stems [pirð-] and [pə̆rɔ̄ð-] are intrepreted as realizing an identical underlying stem shape, |parad|, an interpretation not only compelling in the case of this lexeme, but in fact predicted from a tendential principle of Hebrew morphology: lexical invariance of a nominal stem within its singular or plural subparadigm, though heteroclisis (notably metaplasm or gender-switching) not rarely occurs between such subparadigms.[12]

3.3. Geminate Stops

3.3.1. DIFFICULTIES OF REDUCING THE A-PHONEMIC ANALYSIS TO S-PHONEMIC TERMS

A. Note that the morphologic relation incidentally illustrated by (3a) [dɔ̄vɔ̄́r] and (4e) [haddɔ̄vɔ̄́r] is absolutely general: a stem-initial [P] systematically alternates with [PP] under prefixation with the definite article [ha-] or certain other formatives. In isolation, this suggests that the A-phonemic analysis as (7e-h) /dɔ̄vɔ̄r/ and /hadɔ̄vɔ̄r/ is explanatory of the alternation in question, and hence would be equivalent to positing a low-level S-phonemic rule to the effect that:

(13) A non-pharyngealized simplex stop is geminated intervocalically.

But this prima facie appearance of A-phonemic and S-phonemic accord vanishes with the attempt to integrate (13) into the whole of Tiberian morphophonology, at least in two ways:

B. Rule (13) is incompatible with rule (8). Both the input description and environment of the former are special cases of those of the latter, but the output changes of the two rules are contradictory. In lieu of [haddɔ̄vɔ̄́r], for example, prior (8) and low-level (13) would give, in association with other rules, incorrect §[hă̆ðɔ̄vɔ̄r]; while the converse ordering would predict equally incorrect §[haddabbɔ̄r].

C. Independently of §3.3.2, the alternational patterning adduced in §3.3.1.A. is more general than the purview of A-phonemic rule (7e-h), since ANY non-low consonant--not merely a *begedkefet* stop--is geminated under prefixation with the definite article [ha-] or the other relevant formatives; e.g. (1a) [nɔ̄hɔ̄r] vis-à-vis (2e) [hannɔ̄hɔ̄r]. But the discussion in §2 showed that the A-phonemic analysis of these forms must be respectively (7a) /nɔ̄hɔ̄r/ and (7b) /hannɔ̄hɔ̄́r/.

---

[12]One minor exception to this principle involves several singular stems of unmarked shape |CaCiC| but with construct (morphosyntactically proclitic) shape |CaCC|; cf. Bauer & Leander (1962:552). Incidentally, the fact that stem-shape variance is relatively common between singular and plural happens to be exemplified by |parad| whose corresponding singular is |pard| (in part symptomized by the non-spirantalization of [d] in (3g) [happirdɔ̄]; for the corresponding masculine (5c) [happɛ̄rɛð], cf. Malone 1972:§3.5). In fact, it is normal for Hebrew nouns of singular shape $|CV_x CC|$ to select plurals of shape $|CV_x aC|$.

D. The preceding considerations lead to the conclusion that (13) cannot be an S-rule, both because the environment (intervocalic position) is incorrect and because the input description (*begedkefet* stops) is too narrow. This is not to deny, however, that relations such as [dɔ̄vɔ̄́r, haddɔ̄vɔ̄́r], [nɔ̄hɔ̄́r, hannɔ̄hɔ̄́r], and a variety of other alternations, make inevitable the recognition of gemination as the output of some genuine S-phonemic process. In fact, a thorough treatment would require postulation of several S-phonemic origins of gemination, of which it will be useful to discuss only three in this paper: two quite summarily (§3.3.2.A-B) and one in a bit more detail (§3.3.2.C).

3.3.2. THE S-PHONEMIC ANALYSIS IN ITS OWN TERMS

A. The gemination illustrated in [hannɔ̄hɔ̄́r] and [haddɔ̄vɔ̄́r] occurs, in all clear cases, following a handful of prefixes and proclitics of phonetic shape [CV-], most or all of which however may derive historically from shape *CV̆C-.[13] Though diachronically gemination in such cases may have originated from total assimilation of the Auslaut of *CV̆C- to the stem-initial consonant, continued synchronic existence of the relevant *C-s cannot be postulated, the descriptive economy of the new system being perhaps best captured by attributing, via minor rule, stem-initial gemination to the specific prefixes and proclitics themselves. This effect will be informally abbreviated below by |XC|, where |C| = the stem-initial consonant.

B. Total assimilation of *n* under various conditions to an immediately following consonant, with alternational preservation of that *n* in non-preconsonantal environments. Such assimilation clearly comprises a major rule in the case of 1√*n* (i.e., first radical *n*) and an immediately following non-low consonant; with root √*npl*- contrast prevocalic 1√*n* in (1c) [nɔ̄fā́l] with preconsonantal 1√*n* in |yinpṓl| → |yippṓl|.

C. Though distinct in derivational origin, the several geminational processes converge in phonetic output. S-phonemically this suggests that their ordering relations to other rules are effectively identical, while A-phonemically it has the consequence that the analysis of gemination is quite independent of morphophonemic correlation (with the qualification of note 6). For reasons that will become clear in §4.1, this pair of observations will make it useful to describe just one more kind of gemination: a limiting case of pre-phonological introduction such that phonetic geminate clusters stand in a one-to-one relation with corresponding clusters on the systematic phonemic level itself.[14] An example is provided by feminine abstract nouns of underlying stem shape |CiCC| with geminate roots (those with identical 2√ and 3√): e.g. with root √*zmm*, (2e) [zimmɔ̄́]; with √*mdd*, (4e) [middɔ̄́]. The hypothesis that the corresponding underlying stem shapes are |zimm| and |midd| is supported by several converging lines of evidence, three of which will be mentioned here. (i) Strong (morphophonemically unmarked) roots also evidence phonetic [CiCC], e.g. (3g) [(lə̆)rixbɔ̄́] with root √*rkb*, which supports the analysis of the relevant geminate clusters ([mm] and [dd]) as compositely manifesting 2√ and 3√. (ii) The underlying components of [mm] ([dd]) are specifically 2√*m* and 3√*m* (2√*d* and 3√*d*), as is evidenced by the independent phonetic manifestation of these radicals in homoparadigmatic forms like (1c) [zɔ̄mā́m] and (5e) [mɔ̄ðā́ð]; cf.

---

[13]Our corpus incidentally illustrates another of these proclitics, the so-called *waw consecutive* [wa-] in (1e) [wattɛ̄́mɛr], which following the persuasive analysis of Hetzron (1969: 9) derives from **way*-. (Other suggested origins include < **wal*- [Schramm 1957] and < just plain **wa*- [Bauer & Leander 1962:218]).

[14]Presupposed, however, is the characteristically Semitic process of stem-building by intercalation of usually vocalic functor morphemes or SCHEMES within consonantal contentive morphemes or ROOTS. This process was rather thoroughly formalized for another Semitic language in Malone (1967) by so-called THEMATIC SYMBOLIZATION RULES (pp. 125-38) followed by a special AMALGAMATION RULE (pp. 135-8). In the spirit of Chomsky & Halle (1968), at least the latter should constitute a READJUSTMENT RULE (ibid. pp. 9-11).

also strong (1a) [rɔ̄xāv]. (iii) Underlying |CiCC|, the apriori best hypothesis given its isomorphism to [CiCC], simply encounters no viable alternative. Of particular importance here is the observation that an underlying vowel between 2√ and 3√ would at a minimum effect Spirantalization (8) of a *begedkefet* 3√ and would moreover in most cases be itself preserved by Pretonic Lengthening (11); e.g. an underlying stem |rikab| would give §[rəxɔ̄vɔ̄] instead of actual [rixbɔ̄] (cf. derivation (12)).

The relevant aspects of the S-phonemic derivation of [middɔ̄] are thus:

(14) (...) |middā|
(8,11,9 do not apply) -
(---) [middɔ̄]

The crucial point, for reasons that will become clear in §4.1, is that [dd] is not the product of a phonological rule: it is present from the start.[15]

(15) The S-phonemic analysis in summary, row-wise calibrated with the A-phonemic analysis of (7):

(a) |M| → [M]. E.g. (1a) [nɔ̄hɔ̄r].
(b) |XM| → [MM]. E.g. (2e) [hannɔ̄hɔ̄r] (§3.3.5).
(c) |nM| → [MM]. E.g. (2e) [tiqqōm] (§3.3.6).
(d) |MM| → [MM]. E.g. (2e) [zimmɔ̄] (§3.3.7).
(e) |XP| → [PP]. E.g. (4e) [haddɔ̄vɔ̄r] (§3.3.5).
(f) |nP| → [PP]. E.g. (4e) [yippōl] (§3.3.6).
(g) |PP| → [PP]. E.g. (4e) [middɔ̄] (§3.3.7).
(h) |P| → [P] /normally. E.g. (3a) [dɔ̄vɔ̄r] (§3.2).
(i) |P| → [F] /postvocalically. E.g. (5g) [pirəēhɛ̄m] (§3.2).
(j) §[FF] is blocked by condition of rule (8), as well as by the special condition on rule (9) stated in note 10.

4. IRRECONCILABLE INCOMPATIBILITY OF THE A-PHONEMIC AND S-PHONEMIC ANALYSES

4.1. A-phonemics Must Cede

The considerations of §§2-3 have shown that A-phonemic and S-phonemic analyses of Tiberian Hebrew are not isomorphic. This is not surprising, of course, but what we want to ascertain

[15]Clarification of a minor point which could wax major if not correctly interpreted: reference to the PHONETIC strings as "geminate" and use of the corresponding transcription [CC] must NOT be understood as opposed to "long" and [C·] resp. Indeed, available evidence certainly points to a non-interrupted pronunciation of the Tiberian [CC]'s, as in those contemporary Semitic languages where merger with simplices has not taken place. Use of the term "gemination" and the representation [CC] in this paper was chosen both to obviate the superfluity of symbological repercussions which another choice would have entailed, and also as a concession to Semitistic convention. See also note 16a.

now is whether these analyses are even mutually compatible. If they are, in the orthodox sense, then from any S-phonemic derivation it ought to be possible to isolate at least one line isomorphic (in relevant respects) to the corresponding A-phonemic structure of the form in question. This is possible in four out of five of the A-phonemic solutions presented in (7), as can be seen in the following:

(16)	(a)	(...)	|nahā́r|
		(8 does not apply)	-
		(11)	nāhā́r
		(9 d.n.a.)	-
		(---)	[nɔ̄hɔ̄́r] = /nɔ̄hɔ̄́r/
	(b-d)	(...)	|zimmā́|
		(8,9,11 d.n.a.)	-
		(---)	[zimmɔ̄́] = /zimmɔ̄́/
	(e-h)	See (17-18).	
	(i) (= 10)	(...)	|paradēhḗm|
		(8)	paraðēhḗm
		(11 d.n.a.)	-
		(9)	parðēhḗm
		(---)	[pirðēhḗm] = /pirðēhḗm/

But in the case of /P/, the compatibility holds only in the case of [P]:

(17) (cf. 7h)	(...)	|dabā́r|
	(8)	davā́r
	(11)	dāvā́r
	(9 d.n.a.)	-
	(---)	[dɔ̄vɔ̄́r] = /dɔ̄vɔ̄́r/

but not in the case of [PP]:

(18) (=14; cf. 7e-g)	(...)	|middā́| ≠ /midɔ̄́/
	(8,11,9 d.n.a.)	-
	(---)	[middɔ̄́] ≠ /midɔ̄́/

Of course it would be possible to change the S-phonemic analysis by adding a low-level rule like this:

(19) A non-pharyngealized geminate stop cluster is simplified intervocalically.[16]

---

[16]Technically, the qualification "intervocalically" is superfluous. But this redundancy will sharpen the contour of subsequent discussion in various ways.

with the effect that (18) is replaced by:

(20)	(...)	|middā́|
	(8,11,9 d.n.a.)	-
	(---)	middɔ̄́
	(19)	[midɔ̄́] = /midɔ̄́/

But (20) is simply incorrect, because the last line of an S-phonemic derivation must be SYSTEMATIC PHONETIC, i.e. here [middɔ̄́], which the (19)-derived anomaly §[midɔ̄́] is not. Thus (19) would have to be followed by an even lower level rule, equivalent to A-phonemic subrule (7e):

(21) A non-pharyngealized simplex stop is geminated intervocalically.

with the effect that (20) would be replaced by:

(22)	(...)	|middā́|
	(8,9,11 d.n.a.)	-
	(---)	middɔ̄́
	(19)	midɔ̄́ = /midɔ̄́/
	(21)	[middɔ̄́]

But (22), *per se* and as representative of an S-phonemic analysis of [PP] in general, is preposterous since the last and third-to-last lines are identical (both *middɔ̄́*) BY DEFINITION of rule (21), THE NECESSARY AND SUFFICIENT CONDITIONS OF WHOSE APPLICATION ARE TO UNDO THE APPLICATION OF RULE (19), which all means that rule (19) effectively does not exist. The conclusion is unescapable that the only rationale for (19) is to force a counterfactual compatibility of the S-phonemic and A-phonemic analyses in question, and that the actual S-phonemic analysis is faithfully represented by derivation (18), where its inherent incompatibility with the A-phonemic analysis is undisguised.

4.2. Comparison with Analogous Cases in the Literature

The case of S- vs. A-phonemic incompatibility just documented is markedly more radical than the classic cases of Turkish adduced by Lees (1957:389f) and Russian adduced by Halle (1971: 22f). These simply involved partial duplication of labor: the phenomenon of final devoicing was accounted for S-phonemically for certain segments and A-phonemically for others, while a pure-state S-phonemic analysis could provide a unitary account. But in the Tiberian case just documented the duplication of labor in accounting for gemination is not merely partial, it is complete: (21) covers all and only the cases accounted for by genuine S-phonemic rules and patterns (e.g. §3.3.2); and this absurd situation is aggravated by and in fact dependent upon the postulation of a *deus ex machina*, (19), whose only role is to create conditions for (21). The analogs of (19) and (21) cited by Lees and Halle were real rules, merely not as general as they might be. But (19) and (21) are pseudo-rules, whose net effect is to cancel each other out.

The stark difference between the Turnish and Russian cases on the one hand and the Tiberian case on the other is also revealed by the interactability of the latter to various attempted challenges to Lees' and Halle's treatment of the former. E.g. Ferguson's claim (1962 in Makkai 1972:372) that in the Turkish case the relevant S-phonemic and A-phonemic devoicing rules "are quite different in the phonological and grammatical structure of the language" is not transferrable to Tiberian S-phonemic and A-phonemic accounts of *begedkefet* gemination since, as has just been pointed out, A-phonemic (21) covers all and only the cases accounted for by S-phonemic rules and patterns such as §3.3.2. Nor will the tack work of hypostatizing a segment (Sydney M. Lamb cited by Postal 1968:39-41) or feature (Lockwood 1972:193-4) representing the opposition neutralized and then deleting that segment or feature by a morphophonemic rule in the neutralizational environment: because in the Tiberian case THIS IS PRECISELY WHAT RULE (19) ACHIEVES and yet, as we have seen, the phonetic facts require restitution of the relevant geminates by (21). Finally, Schane's recent proposal (1971) fails to rescue the A-phonemic analysis of (7) for the simple reason that his explication requires the isolation from any S-phonemic derivation of at least one line to be defined as "phonemic," but we have already seen (§4.1) that this will not work with Tiberian gemination if by "phonemic" is meant "A-phonemic."[16a]

5. THE APPARENT A-PHONEMIC FUNCTION OF THE GRAPHEME *dagesh*

It would be possible for this paper to conclude to the tune of §4.2, and so simply to comprise yet another piece of evidence against autonomous phonology. But the Tiberian orthography presents evidence that the Masoretes (see note 1) who devised the relevant portion of the writing system, i.e. the diacritical POINTING SYSTEM supplementing the received consonantal orthography, did in fact analyze consonant relations very much along the lines of the A-phonemic analysis of (7). Consider in column I of (23) the orthographic representations of the types of phonetic consonantism in column II, each such type correlated with its A-phonemic analysis in column III (cf. 7) and its S-phonemic analysis in column IV (cf. 15). Note now that every geminate cluster, (b-g), is marked by the grapheme *dagesh*, in the form of a dot modifying the corresponding consonant letter. On the other hand simplices are represented by unmodified consonantal letters, with one exception: The *begedkefet* stops (h) [P] are marked with *dagesh* identically to their homorganic geminates (e-g) [PP], WHICH AGREES PRECISELY WITH THE A-PHONEMIC ANALYSIS OF THESE SOUNDS and moreover makes no sense in either phonetic or S-phonemic terms. In fact, the A-phonemic interpretation holds for the entire cross-section of the Tiberian consonant system considered in this paper: note in (23) that column I stands in a one-to-one relation only to column III.[18]

[16a]Sampson (1973) has recently adduced evidence in all likelihood interpretable to the effect that the difference between CC and C· touched upon in note 15 above is relevant not only to pronunciation but even to the very heart of Hebrew phonology, and since despite one or two reservations I tend to agree with him and have in fact attempted to show that his hypothesis should be at least in part instrumented by a Melding rule CC → C· ordered before Spirantalization (Malone, forthcoming), it will be important to clarify that these adjustments do not substantively affect the arguments made in the present paper. The formal effect of Sampson's insight on the S-phonemic analysis of §3 is, as said, inclusion of Melding to be ordered before Spirantalization, while the impact on the A-phonemic analysis of §2 would be adjustment of rule (7e) to /P/ → [P·] / V__V. But the joint effect of these adjustments is merely to recast cardinal derivation (18) as follows:

(18')	(...)	|middā́|	≠	/midɔ̄́/
	(Melding)	mid·ā́	≠	/midɔ̄́/
	(8,11,9 d.n.a)	-		
	(---)	[mid·ɔ̄́]	≠	/midɔ̄́/

and to rephrase pseudo-S-rules (19) and (21) in terms of length rather than gemination. I am grateful to C. Douglas Johnson for calling Sampson's paper (1973) to my attention.

[17]For details cf. Paul Kahle *apud* Bauer & Leander (1962:56-162) and Bergsträsser (1962: I 28-81).

[18]The brief discussion of §5 admittedly wrenches the role of *dagesh* from the full context of Tiberian orthography, and at least a few questions may be anticipated from those familiar

(23)	I	II	III	IV
(a)	< M >	[M]	/M/	|M|
(b)	< $\mathring{M}$ >	[MM]	/MM/	|XM|
(c)	< $\mathring{M}$ >	[MM]	/MM/	|nM|
(d)	< $\mathring{M}$ >	[MM]	/MM/	|MM|
(e)	< $\mathring{P}$ >	[PP]	/P/	|XP|
(f)	< $\mathring{P}$ >	[PP]	/P/	|nP|
(g)	< $\mathring{P}$ >	[PP]	/P/	|PP|
(h)	< $\mathring{P}$ >	[P]	/P/	|P|
(i)	< P >	[F]	/F/	|P|

6. A SOLUTION TO THE PARADOXICAL CONFLICT OF §§ 4-5

6.1. David Johns' Explication of A-phonemic Functions

If the facts and interpretations presented throughout above are sufficiently real and accurate, we must fact the question of the individual merits and joint compatibility of the following claims:

(24) (a) A-phonemics is included in S-phonemics in the sense that while both structurally analyze speech sounds, only S-phonemics is responsible to morphophonemic patterning.

(b) But the A-phonemic analysis of (7) and the S-phonemic analysis of (15) are incompatible.

(c) Therefore (7) is inferior to (15).

(d) But the orthography contains patterning (of *dagesh*) that is only understandable in terms of (7).

(e) Therefore the orthography is inferior.

---

with this writing system: (i) The Masoretes may have used the same dot for [P] and [PP], but they called the former *dagesh lene* (קל) and the latter *dagesh forte* (חזק); hence we are dealing with mere homography. But in fact the Masoretes apparently did *not* recognize this distinction, which originated later with the medieval grammarian Joseph Ḳimḥi (Chomsky 1952:374 note 32a; cf. also Kautzsch 1910:55 note 1). (ii) *Dagesh* has other usages (e.g. so-called *dagesh conjunctivum*, *dagesh dirimens*) not obviously reducible to the suggested A-phonemic representation. True, but this seems simply to mean that the proposed A-phonemic function was one of a family of functions invested in *dagesh* by the Masoretes--which is not to deny that the rationale(s) for just this family of functions are not fully understood. But the interpretation that *dagesh* served more than one function should *per se* court no suspicion: cf. the use of capitalization in English orthography to mark proper names, sentential Anlaut, etc. (iii) The relevant orthography is not exclusively A-phonemic; in particular, (23h-i) פּ < $\mathring{P}$ > and פ < P > in abstraction of *dagesh* reveal the same grapheme פ < P > answering to the unity of S-phonemic |P| rather than to the distinction of A-phonemic /P/ ≠ /F/. True, but this is perfectly compatible with the position of this paper, which is merely that the distribution of *dagesh* is only A-phonemically but not also S-phonemically interpretable. Moreover, the relevant use of פ < P > is actually HISTORICAL SPELLING, a fait accompli of the pre-Tiberian orthography which the Masoretes for religious reasons were not at liberty to tamper with.

Now I would like to take the position that while (b) and (d) are true, yet (a) is a half-truth whose mendacious side disqualifies immediately conclusion (c) and mediately conclusion (e). In particular, I submit that A-phonemics is NOT NECESSARILY included in S-phonemics because their structural analyses of speech sounds are NOT NECESSARILY of the same type. The qualification "not necessarily" must be emphasized because the new-Bloomfieldian structural theory of language, of which A-phonemics is a subtheory, has never been sufficiently developed to allow of explicit, formal comparison with the generative theory of language, of which S-phonemics is a subtheory. So the important point here is that proposition (a) ignores the fact that A-phonemics CAN AND PERHAPS SHOULD BE EXPLICATED TO PROVIDE A STRUCTURAL ANALYSIS OF SPEECH SOUNDS DISTINCT FROM THE S-PHONEMIC. Nor does this idea originate with me. Various scholars of various adherences have at least intimated acceptance of such a position, though few full and explicit statements have come to my attention and amongst those that have, at least Schane's (1971) fails to explicate the A-phonemic analysis in question here, as we saw in §4.2. On the other hand, the proposal of Johns (1969) not only works but rings true. Briefly, he proposes that at least a major function of A-phonemics be explicated as the representation of NEUTRALIZATION, and that within a generative framework such neutralization be formalized by *feature-deletion rules* and, crucially, that the A-phonemic and S-phonetic levels *constitute parallel terminal derivations from S-phonemic inputs*, as in the following figure:

(25)

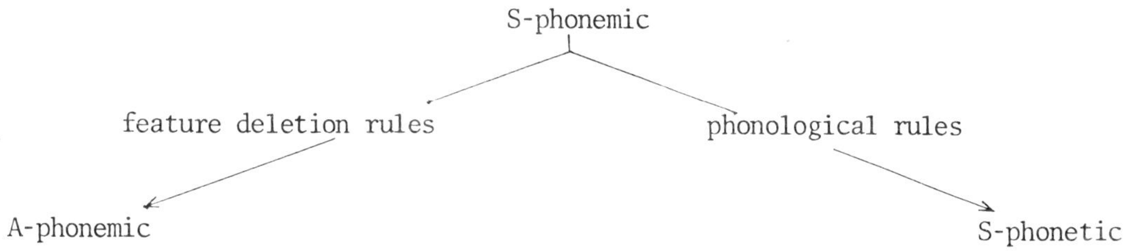

In the case of Tiberian gemination, the problematic example of [middɔ̄́] (§4.1) would find the resolution of (26), where |middā́| → /midɔ̄́/ wpi;d be accommodated by a rule deleting gemination in the case of *begedkefets*, thus formalizing the neutralization of the distinctivity of gemination in the case of these sounds. This rule of degemination can in fact be viewed as (19), now decontaminated from association with pseudo-rule (21) whose necessity vanishes as soon as /midɔ̄́/ ceases to be viewed as an intermediary step in the derivation of [middɔ̄́] from |middā́|.[19]

(26)

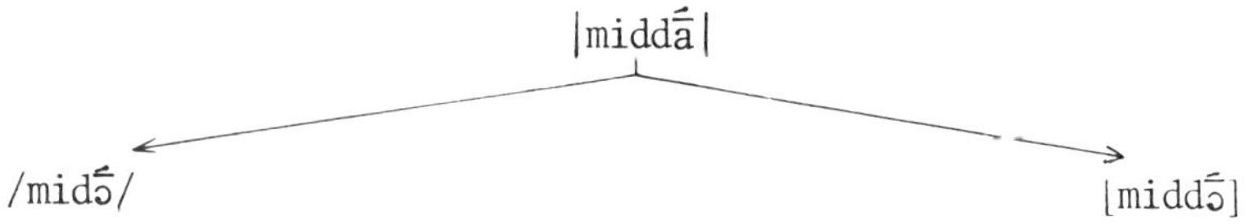

[19] Formal representability of connectedness of sorts distinct from steps-in-a-derivation has not been invested by generative theoreticians with an amount of attention commensurate to the importance of such representability in capturing certain facets of language patterning. On the other hand, I lay aside reservations of other sorts to suggest that this is one area where stratificational linguistics shows some success, in particular in the area of what they call TACTICS. Without elaboration, I submit here a cross-section of a hypothetical stratificational network (based on Lockwood 1972) showing how TACTICS right-hand side) might relate the analog of A-phonemic /P/ to the analog of S-phonemic |PP| (upper left-hand side) without messing with the derivational trip of the latter towards phonetic [PP] (lower left-hand side). However, this is not to claim that a stratificationalist would accommodate these specific Tiberian relations in just this way: though stratification-

6.2. Conclusion

Acceptance of an explication of A-phonemics like Johns' undermines hypothesis (24a)--since rather than S-phonemics and A-phonemics standing in a relation of inclusion they emerge as partially independent coordinate analyses--and thus disqualifies conclusion (24c) that the A-phonemic analysis of (7) must be inferior to the S-phonemic analysis of (15). Moreover in this light the observation of (24d) not only fails to lead to the damning conclusion of (24e), but contrariwise may even be interpreted as independent evidence for the bona fides of the specific A-phonemic analysis of (7). Since the Masoretes who devised the relevant part of the orthography (§5) evidenced extraordinary scrupulosity and thoroughness, such a conclusion seems well warranted. But *why* did the Masoretes choose this sort of representation? And in particular why didn't they choose to capture deeper sorts of cohesion which we might call S-phonemic? A likely answer has been long recognized by Hebraists and Judaists: the most crucial benefice in devising the relevant part of the orthography, the so-called POINTING, was to ENSURE CORRECT PRONUNCIATION AND CANTILLATION OF THE HOLY SCRIPTURES. Hence in the case of conflicting possibilities, as with gemination, it was more important to ensure accurate pronunciation than accurate portrayal of morphophonological relations, AND AN A-PHONEMIC ORTHOGRAPHY IS EMINENTLY APPROPRIATE TO SUCH A PURPOSE. Significantly, just such a conclusion for the general orthographic-phonologic relation was reached by King (1969:212) quite independently of Tiberian Hebrew or any other Semitic data.

BIBLIOGRAPHY

Bauer, Hans & Pontus Leander. 1962 [orig.1922]. *Historische Grammatik der hebräischen Sprache des Alten Testamentes*. Hildesheim: Olms.

Bergsträsser, Gotthelf. 1962 [orig.1918-1929]. *Hebräische Grammatik*, I and II. Hildesheim: Olms.

Brame, Michael K. 1971. "Stress in Arabic and generative phonology," *FL* 7.556-91.

Cantineau, J. 1950. "Essai d'une phonologie de l'hébreu biblique," *BSLP* 46.82-122.

Chomsky, Noam & Morris Halle. 1968. *The sound pattern of English*. New York et alibi: Harper & Row.

Chomsky, William. 1952. *David Kimḥi's Hebrew Grammar (Mikhlol)*. New York: Bloch.

Ferguson, Charles A. 1962. Review of Halle 1971. *Lg*. 38.284-98. [Reprinted in Makkai 1972:369-79].

alists have been amongst the staunchest defenders of something akin to the A-phoneme, yet their explications are not really appreciable outside the full context of their theory and highly specialized model.

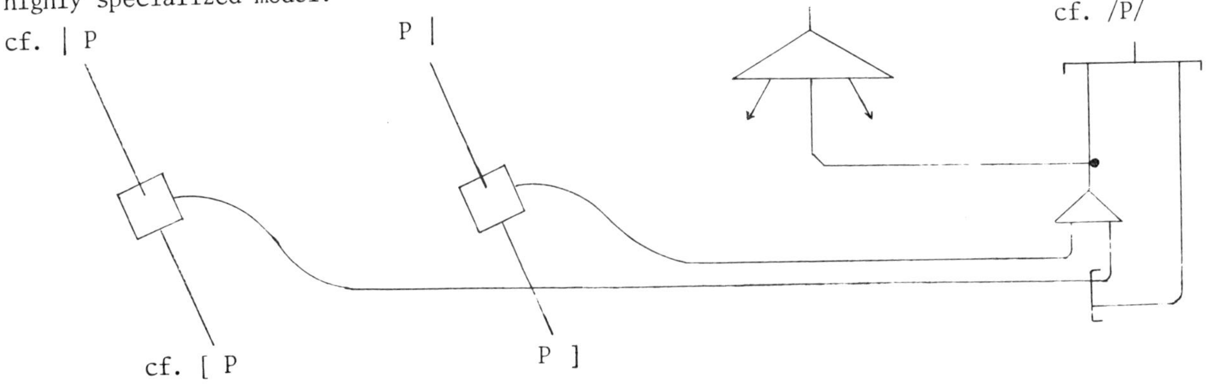

Halle, Morris. 1971 [orig.1959]. *The sound pattern of Russian.* The Hague: Mouton.

Harris, Zellig S. 1941. "Linguistic structure of Hebrew," *JAOS* 61.143-67.

Hetzron, Robert. 1969. "The evidence for perfect **y'aqtul* and jussive **yaqt'ul* in proto-Semitic," *JSS* 14.1-21.

Johns, David A. 1969. "Phonemics and generative phonology," *Papers from the Fifth Regional Meeting of the Chicago Linguistic Society*, 374-81. Chicago: University of Chicago Linguistics Department. [Reprinted in Makkai 1972:549-53].

Kautzsch, E.(ed.). 1910. *Gesenius' Hebrew Grammar* (revised by A. E. Cowley). Oxford: Clarendon.

King, Robert D. 1969. *Historical linguistics and generative grammar.* Englewood Cliffs: Prentice-Hall.

Kittel, R. et al.(eds.). 1971. *Biblia Hebraica.* Stuttgart: Württembergische Bibelanstalt Stuttgart.

Kuryłowicz, Jerzy. 1959. "Accentuation of the verb in Indo-European and in Hebrew," *Word* 15.123-9.

Lees, Robert B. 1957. Review of Syntactic structures, by Noam Chomsky. *Lg.* 33.375-408.

Lockwood, David G. 1972. *Introduction to stratificational linguistics.* New Yory et alibi: Harcourt Brace Jovanovich.

Makkai, Valerie Becker(ed.). 1972. *Phonological theory: evolution and current practice.* New York et alibi: Holt, Rinehart & Winston.

Malone, Joseph L. 1967. *A morphologic grammar of the Classical Mandaic verb*, Univ. California (Berkeley) Ph.D. diss. Ann Arbor: University Microfilms.

_______________. 1969. "Rules of synchronic analogy: a proposal based on evidence from three Semitic languages," *FL* 5.534-59.

_______________. 1972. "A Hebrew flip-flop rule and its historical origins," *Lingua* 30. 422-448.

_______________. Forthcoming. "Messrs. Sampson, Chomsky & Halle, and the Hebrew phonology," to appear in *Foundations of Language.*

Morag, Shelomo. 1962. *The vocalization systems of Arabic, Hebrew, and Aramaic.* The Hague: Mouton.

Postal, Paul M. 1968. *Aspects of phonological theory.* New York et alibi: Harper & Row.

Sampson, Geoffrey. 1973. "Duration in Hebrew consonants," *Linguistic Inquiry* 4.101-104.

Schane, Sanford A. 1971. "The phoneme revisited," *Lg.* 47.503-21.

Schramm, Gene M. 1957. "A reconstruction of Biblical Hebrew waw consecutive," *GL* 3.1-8.

_______________. *The graphemes of Tiberian Hebrew.* Berkeley et alibi: University of California.

Wang, William S-Y. 1968. "Vowel features, paired variables, and the English vowel shift," *Lg.* 44.695-708.

FIRST NORTH-AMERICAN CONFERENCE ON SEMITIC LINGUISTICS

Santa Barbara, California
March 24-25, 1973

The first North-American Conference on Semitic Linguistics was organized by Robert Hetzron (University of California, Santa Barbara) with the cooperation of Giorgio Buccellati (University of California, Los Angeles) and Joseph L. Malone (Barnard College--Columbia University). The purpose of the Conference is to promote the interest of Semitists in the various modern currents of linguistics. The full list of the papers presented at the 1973 Conference is given below. Those papers which have been submitted and accepted for inclusion in *AAL*, like the present one, are being published within the framework of the journal.

A. *Semitic and its Afroasiatic Cousins*

1. Carleton T. Hodge (University of Indiana), *The Nominal Sentence in Semitic* (=*AAL* 2/4).
2. G. Janssens (University of Ghent, Belgium), *The Semitic Verbal System* (=*AAL* 2/4).
3. J. B. Callender (UCLA), *Afroasiatic Cases and the Formation of Ancient Egyptian Verbal Constructions with Possessive Suffixes* (=*AAL* 2/6).
4. Russell G. Schuh (UCLA), *The Chadic Verbal System and its Afroasiatic Nature* (forthcoming in *AAL*).
5. Andrzej Zaborski (University of Cracow, Poland), *The Semitic External Plural in an Afroasiatic Perspective* (forthcoming in *AAL*).

B. *Ancient Semitic Languages*

6. Giorgio Buccellati (UCLA), *On the Akkadian "Attributive" Genitive* (forthcoming in *AAL*).
7. Daniel Ronnie Cohen (Columbia University), *Subject and Object in Biblical Aramaic: A Functional Approach Based on Form-Content Analysis* (=*AAL* 2/1).
8. Richard Steiner (Touro College, N.Y.), *Evidence from a Conditioned Sound Change for Lateral ḏ in Pre-Aramaic.*
9. Stanislav Segert (UCLA), *Verbal Categories of Some Northwest Semitic Languages: A Didactical Approach* (=*AAL* 2/5).
10. Charles Krahmalkov (University of Michigan), *On the Noun with Heavy Suffixes in Punic.*

C. *Hebrew*

11. Joseph L. Malone (Barnard College--Columbia University), *Systematic vs. Autonomous Phonemics and the Hebrew Grapheme "dagesh"* (=*AAL* 2/7).
12. Allan D. Corré (University of Wisconsin, Milwaukee), *"Wāw" and "Digamma"* (forthcoming in *AAL*).
13. Harvey Minkoff (Hunter College, N.Y.), *A Feature Analysis of the Development of Hebrew Cursive Scripts* (=*AAL* 1/7).
14. Raphael Nir (Hebrew University, Jerusalem), *The Survival of Obsolete Hebrew Words in Idiomatic Expressions* (=*AAL* 2/3).
15. Talmy Givón (UCLA), *On the Role of Perceptual Clues in Hebrew Relativization* (=*AAL* 2/8).
16. Alan C. Harris (UCLA), *The Relativization "which that is" in Israeli Hebrew.*

D. *Arabic*

17. Ariel A. Bloch (University of California, Berkeley), *Direct and Indirect Relative Clauses in Arabic.*
18. Frederic J. Cadora (Ohio State University), *Some Features of the Development of Telescoped Words in Arabic Dialects and the Status of Koiné II.*

E. *Ethiopian*

19. Gene B. Gragg (University of Chicago), *Morpheme Structure Conditions and Underlying Form in Amharic* (forthcoming in *AAL*).
20. C. Douglas Johnson (University of California, Santa Barbara), *Phonological Channels in Chaha* (=*AAL* 2/2).
21. Robert Hetzron (University of California, Santa Barbara), *The t-Converb in Western Gurage and the Role of Analogy in Historical Morphology* (=*AAL* 2/2).

F. *Beyond Afroasiatic*

22. Gilbert B. Davidowitz (New York), *Cognate Afroasiatic and Indoeuropean Affixes: Conjugational Person-Markers.*

AFROASIATIC DIALECTS

Afroasiatic Dialects (*AAD*) seeks to provide concise descriptions of individual languages which belong to the Afroasiatic language family. It is primarily directed toward an audience consisting, on the one hand, of students of one or several Afroasiatic languages, and, on the other, of students of linguistics. In these volumes, both these groups should find succinct treatises such as to provide familiarity with the basic structure of the language in question in a comparative perspective. Each description will be comprehensive in scope and sufficiently detailed in exemplification. But at the same time the aim will be to cut through to the essential and to avoid specialized argumentation. The goal then is neither to publish a corpus of exhaustive reference grammars nor to provide a platform for the analytical defense of theoretical questions. In this sense the series is properly data-oriented. Though the authors will necessarily be of a variety of theoretical persuasions and each will have his own set of preferences for presentation, not the least important goal will be to achieve as high a degree as possible of uniformity in structure, and in the conventional signs and terminology used. This being accomplished, the reader should have no difficulty in finding points of resemblance and divergence amongst the languages which concern him with regard to some point of inquiry. The term 'dialects' in the series' title refers not only to modern spoken vernaculars but to historically definable stages of any language of the various branches. Publication of studies of as many such dialects as possible would provide, we feel, both an encouragement to comparative work and a sound documentary base on which alone this work may fruitfully progress.

Authors are invited to observe the following guidelines in preparing volumes for the series: Each volume will contain (a) concise background information on the language (geographical information, writing, brief statement of the language's position within the branch or the branch's position within the family, etc.), (b) main features of the phonology, (c) main features of the morphology, (d) main features of the syntax, (e) a short sample narrative text with word-to-word and free translations, (f) a brief selected bibliography, (g) working definitions of terms, signs and abbreviations used (without presupposing familiarity with descriptive grammars). Beyond these required elements, a study may include (h) a section on lexical and/or semantic points of interest (e.g. lexico-statistic word lists, observations on lexical structure, etc.), (i) a brief section of writing and/or alphabet, (j) appendices on points of particular interest brought up in the basic description (e.g. conjugation tables, resumptive tables, historical information, etc.).

AAD 1 - **Berber**

TAMAZIGHT OF THE AYT NDHIR by Thomas G. Penchoen. 1973, IV-124 pp., $8.50.

The Ayt Ndhir dialect which is described belongs to one of the major Berber languages, Tamazight, spoken in the Middle Atlas Mountains of central Morocco. The description is based in the main on research undertaken with native speakers of the Ayt Ndhir territory surrounding El Hajeb.

While directed to the non-specialist, a number of points in the description proper will be of interest to the specialist as well: the presentation of noun and verb morphology points up a number of regularities which more often than not have been obscured in previous descriptions. Also, phonological rules are given which account for the major share of morphophonemic complexities. The reader will find in the appendices and 'optional' sections (see the description of the series given above) conjugation tables of typical verbs–including detailed observations on the placement of shwa in verbs–, a chart showing the main morphological patterns involved in verb derivation, a description of the phonological patterns involved in verb derivation, a description of the phonological rules applying in complex sequences of morphemes of the verb group, the 'basic' vocabulary contained in several well-known lexicostatistic word lists, and a chart of the Tifinaγ alphabet used by the Tuareg.

AAD 2 - **Ancient Egyptian**

MIDDLE EGYPTIAN by John Callender. 1975, 150 pp., $10.

AAD 3 - **Semitic**

DAMASCUS ARABIC by Arne Ambros. In preparation.

All prices are postpaid. Payment must accompany orders from individuals.
A handling fee of 70¢ will be charged to libraries if order is not prepaid. **Institutional and professional discount of 20% through June 30, 1976.**

Order from: **UNDENA PUBLICATIONS, P.O.B. 97, Malibu, California 90265, U.S.A.**

AFROASIATIC LINGUISTICS

Volume One

1. P. Newman and R. G. Schuh, *The Hausa Aspect System*, 38 pp.
2. J. L. Malone, *The Development of the Anomalous Syriac Verb* eškāḥ *'To Find': A Case of Convergent Factors in Linguistic Change,* 10 pp.
3. R. Hetzron, *Extrinsic Ordering in Classical Arabic,* 25 pp.
4. T. Givón, *Verb Complements and Relative Clauses: A Diachronic Case Study in Biblical Hebrew,* 22 pp.
5. T. M. Johnstone, *The Modern South Arabian Languages,* 29 pp.
6. B. W. Andrzejewski, *Indicator Particles in Somali,* 69 pp.
7. H. Minkoff, *Graphemics and Diachrony: Some Evidence from Hebrew Cursive,* 16 pp.

Volume Two

1. D. R. Cohen, *Subject and Object in Biblical Aramaic: A Functional Approach Based on Form-Content Analysis,* 23 pp.
2. C. D. Johnson, *Phonological Channels in Chaha,* 13 pp.
   R. Hetzron, *The t-Converb in Western Gurage (The Role of Analogy in Historical Morphology),* 12 pp.
3. A. Barnea, *Reference to Time, Space and Other Types of Quantification in the City Dialect of Gaza,* 10 pp.
   R. Nir, *The Survival of Obsolete Hebrew Words in Idiomatic Expressions,* 7 pp.
4. C. T. Hodge, *The Nominal Sentence in Semitic*, 7 pp.
   G. Janssens, *The Semitic Verbal Tense System*, 6 pp.
5. S. Segert, *Verbal Categories of some Northwest Semitic Languages: A Didactical Approach*, 12 pp.
6. J. B. Callender, *Afroasiatic Cases and the Formation of Ancient Egyptian Constructions with Possessive Suffixes*, 18 pp.
7. J. L. Malone, *Systematic vs. Autonomous Phonemics and the Hebrew Grapheme* Dagesh, 17 pp.
8. T. Givón, *On the Role of Perceptual Clues in Hebrew Relativization*, 17 pp.
9. A. D. Corré, *Wāw and Digamma,* 7 pp.
   Id., *A Suprasegmental Feature of Length in Semitic,* 6 pp.

undena publications

bibliotheca mesopotamica

Primary sources and interpretive analyses for the study of Mesopotamian civilization.

Volume 1. *Old Sumerian and Old Akkadian Texts in Philadelphia chiefly from Nippur.*
Part One: Literary and Lexical Texts and the Earliest Administrative Documents from Nippur.
By AAGE WESTENHOLZ. xii-210 pp., 3 plates. $18.50 (cloth), $12 (paper).

assur

A journal for the study of Assyrian as a dialect of Akkadian and of Assyria as a special aspect of Mesopotamian civilization.

Editors: K.H. DELLER, P. GARELLI, C. SAPORETTI. Subscription $12.50.
Volume 1 includes articles by S. Parpola, C. Saporetti, M. Fales, K. Grayson.

afroasiatic linguistics

A journal devoted to theoretical articles using Afroasiatic material, and to descriptive, historical and comparative studies.

Editor: R. HETZRON. Subscription $12.50.
The first two volumes include articles by P. Newman and R. Schuh, J.L. Malone, B.W. Andrzejewski, T. Givón, T.M. Johnstone, S. Segert, C.T. Hodge, D.R. Cohen, R. Nir, H. Minkoff.

afroasiatic dialects

A series of grammars providing concise descriptions of individual languages within the Afroasiatic family, and directed to scholars and students in the given language areas as well as in linguistics.

Editors: W. LESLAU and T.G. PENCHOEN.
Volume 1 (Berber). *Tamazight of the Ayt Ndhir.*
By T.G. PENCHOEN. 124 pp. $8.50.

sources and monographs on the ancient near east

Shorter fascicles making available original documents in English translation and important studies by modern scholars in the field of history, religion, literature, art and archaeology of the Ancient Near East.

Editor: G. BUCCELLATI. Subscription $10.
The first two volumes include fascicles by A. Falkenstein, B. Landsberger, I.M. Diakonoff, F.R. Kraus, R.I. Caplice, M. Cohen.

other volumes

Approaches to the Study of the Ancient Near East. A Volume of Studies offered to I.J. Gelb.
A collection of 27 articles on current trends and on the potential of new approaches in linguistic, literary, archaeological and historical fields. Edited by G. BUCCELLATI. 338 pp., 2 pl. (=Orientalia NS, Vol. 42, 1-2). $12.50.

A Bibliography of Homeric Scholarship. Preliminary Edition 1930-19
By DAVID W. PACKARD and TANIA MEYERS. vi-184
Almost 4000 titles, listed alphabetically with a topical ... egories.

Professional and institutional discount of 20% on single cop...
All prices are postpaid. Descriptive flyers and information o... copies available on request.

Undena Publications, P.O. Box 97, Malibu, California 90265, U.S.A.